Three Amazing Stories

God Was Crying Yesterday
Gateway To Hell
Traffic Jam To Heaven

By
Ruby Emanuel-Burchette
Author

authorHOUSE®

AuthorHouse™
1663 Liberty Drive
Bloomington, IN 47403
www.authorhouse.com
Phone: 1 (800) 839-8640

Published by AuthorHouse 04/24/2019

ISBN: 978-1-5462-2732-8 (sc)
ISBN: 978-1-5462-2733-5 (e)

THREE AMAZING STORIES
BY
AUTHOR
RUBY EMANUEL-BURCHETTE

"GOD WAS CRYING YESTERDAY"

GATEWAY TO HELL

TRAFFIC JAM TO HEAVEN

These amazing stories will enter in the minds of those who wonder why God is crying. But will understand why the wrong choice will lead them through a gateway to hell. If they live righteous, they will be put on a journey where they will be stuck in the traffic jam to Heaven.

About the Author

Ruby Emanuel-Burchette is a divorced mother of three wonderful children, seven grandchildren, and five great grandchildren. She is the eldest daughter born to Rosetta and James Emanuel. Ruby was born in Miami, Florida, and attended Bethune Elementary, Dorsey Jr. High, Northwestern High, and Mays High Schools, all in the Miami areas.

Immediately upon graduation from Mays High School, she was hired as a PBX operator at the school. A recipient of the "Future Business Leaders of America (FBLA)" Award, she felt that she would excel in many entities of her life. Gaining many notorieties through-out her career, she felt the desire of becoming a Criminal Justice Student to understand the mind-set of criminal activity. Deterring crime is her utmost concern for young people having knowledge of the consequences they will pay for their crimes. She continues to present dialogues at town hall meetings, elementary and high schools, and with her mentees.

Ruby would like for all Americans to become one-united in the good graces of our Lord and Savior Jesus Christ. We must love each other, and not hate. Hatred is not a welcomed in this world; but love conquers all who believe that the love of God is the right path to take. Unbelievers will have to decide if they would end-up permanently in the pit of hell or reside everlasting in the palace.

About the Illustrators

Kayla Ashley Smith

Kayla was seven years old (now 19) when she drew her imaginary illustration of God. She saw the tears of God, and in these tears, she put a set of eyes, in which she saw His sadness. She imagined that God was not happy with most of the events that takes place on this wonderful Earth that He created.

Daryl Burchette, Sr.

Daryl attended art school at the early age of seven in Reston, Virginia. He was gifted with a talent to draw many characters with a vision. Later in life, he became a barber and hair designer. He has a special and superior ability to create the science of art.

"God Was Crying Yesterday"

"HE'S A SPIRIT"

****

Contents

The Goodness of His Creation

The Earth was created by God. He made the sea of waters for living creatures and birds to fly above the Earth. God created all sorts of animals according to their kind. He made great light to govern the day, and lesser light to govern the night. God created clouds, the moon, and the stars in the sky. He was very pleased.

"God wanted the land to produce vegetation, seed-bearing with the greenery of plants, trees, and grass. They would be designed to produce fruits with seeds in it." We all should be grateful for everyone who makes foods available for us. We should give thanks to the farmers and manufacturers, and those who grow, package, and transport food to us. We must always appreciate the hard work they do and the bounty they produce."

How rooted in God are you? If you follow Him, He will send roots into soil near water to bear fruit for you.

"BE GRATEFUL FOR WHAT GOD HAS GIVEN YOU"

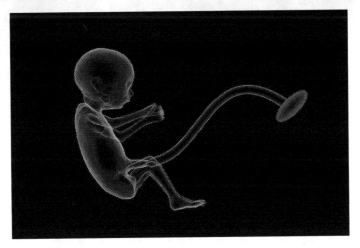

His Loneliness

All that God created was not enough for Him, as He needed to have a conversation with someone whom He could give instructions to. He needed to give directions and guidance to mankind, and in return, He just wanted mankind to be obedient. Therefore, God created man and woman in His own image, and named them Adam and Eve. They lived in a perfect environment. God created them, blessed them, and gave them a beautiful garden to live in. Adam and Eve enjoyed an intimate fellowship with God and each other. They were instructed to be fruitful and multiply the Earth with a generation of families.

"SOW A SEED FOR A GENERATIONAL BLESSING"

Wickedness In The Land

Our Father in Heaven just wanted peace and good will in the land that He created; but He has witnessed turmoil. His creation of mankind and womankind has much displeasure. There's too much division in marriages and families. His sadness at the mistreatment of wives by their mates, often times having illicit love affairs with other women. Adam never mistreated Eve, nor did he leave Eve for another woman. God ordained marriage to be a union to love and respect the vows. When He sees the marriage devoured, He gets very emotional and angry. Husbands and wives owe it to God to honor His ordainment of the marriage; but if you don't, He will chastise you both.

God witness so much crime against the innocent, bitter hatred and malice in the hearts of His people. He cries when there is evilness in the land. He doesn't want us to let evil get the best of us, but conquer evil with good. He doesn't want us to put 'hateness' in our brains, but put 'loveness' in our hearts. His heart bleeds when he witness His little Angels being abused, mistreated, and ultimately murdered at the hands of those who are suppose to love them.

"THE PAIN OF DISCIPLINE IS LESS THAN THE PAIN OF REGRET"

Crime From One City To Another

What are families doing to educate their children? God wants to know why aren't they teaching my word at home and at school? He blessed this earth with goodness and mercy, and the expectation of His people to obey what He set in motion so they can abide by His rules. God sees this disobedience as a set-back from what families should maintain in their belief that with Him, all things are possible. The absence of honoring and pledging Him in sanctuaries, keeping His commandments, and praising Him, leads to crime and destruction. The family cannot survive without His grace and mercy. Crime has spread all over cities for the taking of others' belongings, violating their privacy, and destroying their peace of mind.

Many mayors, city leaders, county commissioners, and school personnel are required to assure that jobs are available for parents and young adults. In this quest for the aforementioned, honest wage earnings can and will alleviate the need to commit senseless crimes in neighborhoods. This will make God happy, for He will be pleased to know that everyone has a purpose and a destiny which is to be self-sufficient.

"YOUR DREAM IS A GLANCE OF YOUR DESTINY"

Discrimination of Humankind

God did not discriminate when He created man and woman. He created all to be treated equal. Women and men are equal in the job market, because they both were educated and gained a wealth of knowledge. He did not mean for one gender to excel to become dominant over the other. Different races were designed by God for identification of culture only. All were to be accepted, respected, and equally given opportunities to reach the level of success. This design was created to have all bond together and become either inventors, artists, mathematicians, civil rights leaders, educators, poets, politicians, doctors, musicians, trailblazers, chemists, dreamers, athletes, historians, authors, and social workers, just to name a few. No one was designed to be discriminated against due to the color of their skin, religion, or natural origin.

The bad choices you make today, can be a down payment for tomorrow's problems. Be a difference-maker and let God's plans grow you.

"YOUR IDENTITY WILL DETERMINE YOUR BEHAVIOR"

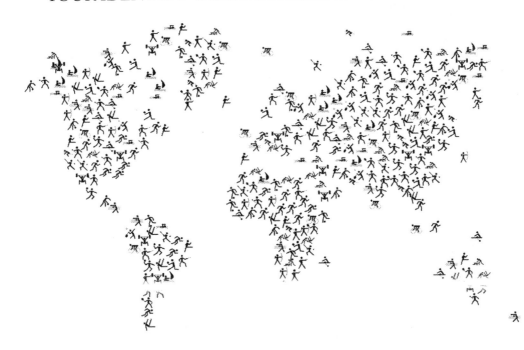

Brotherly Love – Not Hate

There are many tears that stream from God's face. He is witnessing much hatred for fellow mankind that shouldn't be. He loved creating everyone in His own image. No one person should ever hate another, for God loves everyone. He wonders why when He puts His wrath on the Earth, mankind seems to get along and need each other; but when the storm is over, and mankind re-builds and gets re-financed, then all the love and attention diminishes. He's crying because it all seems fake to Him. God doesn't hate on any given day, and He doesn't want His people to hate as well. He wants us to love each other, keep the peace with each other, seek happiness everyday, and share that love through Him. God's love is sufficient for everyone.

"Hatred stirreth up strifes; but love covereth all sins."
Proverbs 10:12

"GOD HAS LAVISHED GREAT LOVE ON US"

14

God's Happy Tears

We, as Americans, must recognize the happy tears that God sheds for us. He is most happy when we appreciate what He has given us. We have freedom to walk or drive on safe streets when we need to arrive at our destination without fear. He has given us the opportunity to gain wealth through earning wages. We have been blessed by Him to worship in houses without persecution. He blessed us to have clean running water to drink; healthy food to eat; gasoline for our cars and lawnmowers; stores to shop; houses to live in; hospitals to heal us from our pain and suffering; a police organization to serve and protect us from harm and danger when we call for help; rain drops for our crops; sunshine to dry-up floods; nightfall when we desire to sleep; and children to love and nurture. We must stay focused on all the blessings of Jesus. We are to thank Him for who He is, what He has done, and for what He can do for us in the future.

While we are on this Earth, God can be found in the midst of our suffering, as He cries with us…He dies with us…and He responds to our tragedies with care. We can be transformed if we think about who He is and how He has remained faithful throughout our lives.

> "Greatly desiring to see thee, being mindful of thy tears, that I may be filled with Joy." II Timothy 1:4

Conclusion

In the conclusion of this short story, it is not intended to insult anyone's religion; however, there is a creator of the universe who sees and knows all that occurs on Earth. Humankind has to be loving, caring, respectful and obedient to God's Commandments.

We all should be concerned about the crime, violence and hatred that takes place in our communities and cities. Let us all be grateful for the many blessings bestowed upon us by our Lord and Savior, Jesus The Christ. He can do the impossible, for He is the Super Natural God.

AMEN

"Gateway To Hell"

AUTHOR
RUBY EMANUEL BURCHETTE

Contents

Introduction

Will Christians experience the wrath of God? It would be the element of surprise should God send you to Hell. Hell is a place where many unsaved individuals will end up. There is a firing furnace. There, sinners will be wailing and gnashing of teeth. The fire will never be quenched. Some believers stated that "The Depictions of Hell is the separation from God; everlasting punishment; a place for spirits and souls; and destruction that has no end." It is my belief that Hell is just a place for those who did not make it into Heaven by God's standards. One must remember that we live life, we expect death, but the judgment seat will be determined by God.

Who Went To Hell?

Lucifer was the fallen angel that God kicked out of Heaven and cast down to Earth. Lucifer roamed the earth seeking whom he could devour. His travels were from nations to nations. He shook the earth and made kingdoms tremble. The world was his wilderness, as he overthrew the cities and held his captives in bondage.

Lucifer was hell-bent on ascending back into Heaven to raise his throne above the stars of God. His greatest desired goal was to be placed on the throne, on the mount of assembly, and the utmost heights of Mount Zaphon. Foolishly, Lucifer wanted to ascend above the tops of the clouds, and make himself the "Most High." How mentally unbalanced he is thinking that he could be the most high. No one on Earth or in Heaven can be seen as the most high (only God is the Most High). Sadly, Lucifer had all these desires; but he ended up into the depths of the pit of hell, and was brought down to the realm of the dead. He was known as the "Morning Star, The Son of the Dawn." His name became a by-word for Satan, and by some, the Devil in the Church.

The Firing Gates of Hell Welcomed Lucifer In

The Firing Gates of Hell

When Lucifer arrived in Hell, he was in a place where he saw fire and brimstone, and the spirits of the dead. He discovered a place where sinners and unbelievers went after death for punishment. Lucifer and many others faced the power of evil and darkness, and knew they just might suffer pain and be treated cruelly. Some may face strict rules that one has to abide to, like never before.

Many will wonder if they will enter into the "Firing Gates of Hell." The determination will be up to God. Good deeds are recognized by God. However, if you do not do good deeds, you will not be given the opportunity to develop them in the eyesight of God. If you are willing to do good deeds, then there's a chance for God to direct your path, which will prevent you from going into the "Pit of Hell." Unlike Lucifer, you may be given the chance of God pulling your card to examine how you lived your life on Earth. God will research your good deeds throughout your life and determine which route you will take… be it Heaven or Hell.

After Satan is Defeated

Satan cannot interfere in the lives of God's people. Hell is everlasting, and souls will continue to be tormented for eternity. Therefore, Christians must exercise the ministry of reconciliation to all in our realm of influence in order to escape damnation.

Put up a fight and let Satan know you're not afraid of him. Laugh at him and not cry. Position yourself as a servant of God, and Satan won't know what will come next.

Conclusion

When you are no longer a prisoner in the pit, you will be rescued, delivered, and given everlasting life. Learn how to walk through a life that is acceptable, and not a journey through the "Gates of Hell." Lace up your shoes for the journey to the "Palace in Heaven." There may be a "Traffic Jam" due to so many escaping the gate of hell.

"MAKING A CHOICE"

LIVE ON EARTH UNDER GOD'S UMBRELLA

"GO TO HELL"

OR

TAKE A JOURNEY TO HEAVEN

"Traffic Jam To Heaven"

[to be added dueing design stage]

SCENES TAKE PLACE THROUGH MANY
TOWNS AND CITIES IN AMERICA
1976

—————◆——✺——◆—————

RUBY EMANUEL-BURCHETTE, AUTHOR

ILLUSTRATIONS
BY
KAYLA ASHLEY SMITH
AND
DARYL BURCHETTE, SR.

Introduction

Ten friends were fed up with life on earth and decided to travel to Heaven to be with God. Life as it was had its limits. These friends met in a specified location in their individual cars and started out on their journey. They drove many miles day and night. On the road, they encountered others wanting to make the same journey.

To their surprise, there were hundreds of ducks headed in the same direction as they were. They could not communicate with the ducks but had the sense to believe they were determined to take that same plight.

The friends became weary and hungry; however, they agreed to go on a 'fast' having nothing but water to drink. They felt that there would be no desire for food in Heaven, that God would supply all their needs.

As they traveled day and night, they witnessed God's creations of the Heavens and the Earth. Never before had they seen such beauty in the mountains, prairie, oceans, rivers, and the sky being so peaceful.

On a very special occasion, they witnessed an eagle giving birth to her babies in her nest. They dared not venture close to the nest in fear of being attacked by the Mother.

Finally, the friends were able to witness two Angels descending from Heaven to take them one by one up in the rapture, an assignment given to them by "The Almighty God."

Contents

Dedication

This book is dedicated in the memory of my many dearly departed loved-ones who were "Heavenly Bound" to be with their Lord and Savior Jesus Christ.

My Dearly Departed Grandmother

Ethel Mae Denmark-Batts-Woodside (2002)

―――――✦――――✵――――✦―――――

My Dear Aunts

Dorothy Woodside (1942)   *Elise Batts-Sorey (2002)*
Essie Batts-Pyron (1977)   *Sarah Batts-Howard (2015)*
Georgetta Batts-Dozier (2000) *Ethel Woodside-Brown (2015)*

―――――✦――――✵――――✦―――――

My Uncle

Johnny Lee Woodside (1994)

―――――✦――――✵――――✦―――――

My Cousins

Altamese Sorey-Cox (2003)   *Michael Sorey, Sr. (2009)*
Clarence Lee Emanuel, Sr. (2005) *Keith Howard (2014)*

―――――✦――――✵――――✦―――――

THOSE WELCOMED INTO THE FAMILY BY MARRIAGE

James A. Emanuel & Thomas Emanuel, Sr.
(June 1972)   *(August 1972)*

Arthur Register, Jr. (1980)   *James Eugene Brown (1996)*
Arthur Henry Sorey, Sr. (1989)   *Willie James Howard, Sr. (2002)*
Eugene Pyron (1996)   *Lawson Leroy Dozier, Sr. (2017)*

a) Miller Mansfield Burchette (1994)
b) Mittie Jones-Burchette (2002)
c) Tannie Eunice (2008)
d) Leroy Pinder (2008)
e) Delmer Stirrup (2018)

SPECIAL DEDICATION TO MY COUSIN
APOSTLE CALVIN C. MILLER, SR. (2017)

"Traffic Jam To Heaven"

Psalm 78:23 – "Though He had commanded the clouds from above, and opened the doors of Heaven"

Chapter 1

"Life On Earth"

Life on earth was getting very bleak. There were plenty of parties, bright lights and many relationships. Living life from day-to-day, wondering how the next life would feel like. Having enjoyed all that I thought was happiness, was nothing but buying grief. Feeling lonely and empty, I felt there must be a road I can travel with nine other friends of mine in the same situation.

As I traveled from place to place observing who was happy and who was not, I noticed people my age seemed to be confused about how they were living. All felt afraid to get into a real relationship in fear of contracting a disease, or getting their hearts broken. They like myself, have been living alone and were definitely set in their ways. We would have choices, cook or eat out; accept dinner invitations or just go to a recreation park and purchase a "sandy hotdog" and an ear of corn on the cob and a soda pop. Oh! Why not take in a movie…eat popcorn and have a large coca cola to escape having to cook. After the movies, its back home to the lonely place; turn on the television and flop down on the plush sofa (guaranteed to fall asleep). When you wake up at 3:00 in the morning (as Lou Rawls would say), you take a visit to the bathroom and return to a lonely bed, unable to go back to sleep. What about some music? It'll put me back to sleep, I thought. While listening to the sounds of Elvis, he sang about the "Hard Headed Woman"; about Adam telling Eve not to eat the darn apple off the tree. Samson told Delilah to keep her fingers out of his curly hair; and how King Ahab was fooling around with Jezebel. Little did I know that Elvis read the Bible.

It is evident that he too knew the goings-on back in Biblical times. Anyway, his music was welcomed by me. Finally, I drifted off to sleep. I began dreaming about living everywhere…where else can I go, I pondered. Having previously lived up the East Coast, maybe I'll go Central. Florida is where I was born and I'm burned out from the heat of the extremely high temperatures. Living up the West Coast introduced me to blizzards, freezing cold days and nights; but still I managed to find the nearest Dairy queen. Early nights, the kids and I would drive up to DQ and find our favorite ice cream. I really liked the banana splits, but the kids liked the DQ bars. Someone in Florida would think that we were nuts (smile). Somehow, I really am afraid of traveling Central USA. There is a lot of snow there (couldn't afford to get snowed in).

Suddenly the telephone rang and awaken me from my dream. When I answered hello, no one was there on the other end of the receiver. I was puzzled because I know I heard the phone ring. As I looked around the room, I realized that I was dreaming and had to chuckle at myself, feeling foolish. When I turned on the light, dispelling the darkness, I saw another day. Well! It's time to get up and shower. Amazingly, I was alert and opened-minded about how I should start my day. It was the same old routine; shower, get dressed and off to work I go. Then, there's the round trip; leave work, drive home, cook dinner or eat out, clean the kitchen and prepare myself for my favorite television programs. I really like dramas; they keep me in suspense. My personal life lacks drama, good drama, so I just tune into the tube. However, the children are always into their own world. They do not bother me.

You would be surprised to know that my nine friends and I are good people who share the same old boring life. We call each other once or twice a month. We chat about what's happening in our cities and what's going on in politics and who died lately. Now, that's really lonely. We all need some excitement in our lives. We are Christians and truly believe in Christ. We are active in Church and serve on an auxiliary at our perspective Churches., whether it be in Florida, Georgia, Alabama, North Carolina, Oklahoma, California, New York, Virginia and the Bahamas. Although we are all in different places, we run up our phone bills expressing our boring existence.

Realizing how bored we are, we concluded that just existing on Earth is not enough and not much of a challenge. What can we do differently? We all had no idea about life after death. We never discussed the rapture, but only heard of it on television programs and various movies. Several months later, we would bring up the subject of the rapture again. The spirit of the minds told us of leaving our loved-ones behind; disappearing from wherever without warnings. We certainly don't want to go to hell. Hell is a place with intense heat and perhaps many enemies unknown. We want to go to Heavenly places to look for new friends, other Christians and best of all, to see Jesus Christ and God Almighty. Perhaps we will see King David and others. Oh! But to dance with King David and listen to him sing. He has so many beautiful "Psalms." Having him recite them would be awesome. The very thought of being in the presence of our Heavenly Father was something greatly desired. Just think, God will give us whatever we sought (happiness, wealth, everlasting life and pure unconditional love). My friends and I desperately want to take that journey to hasten to the throne. What would we have to loose?

On Earth, we're single, lonely and have no young children (they are now all grown up). We were only "built-in Nannies" anyway; so it would be a good time to escape this Earth and journey to Heaven.

After carefully thinking over this mass exit, we imagined the happiness, joy and delight being in the company of our Lord and Savior. There will be many Heavenly places to explore. God will open up the Heavens when we get there. So we're going up yonder. The question is: "how will we get there?" We can't fly there, but we are told that there may be a private road we could take. Private road? Where? Where? That is the big question. One friend refused to walk, but another friend suggested that we each drive our own car. We would number these cars so not to get confused with other cars on our journey and paint them different colors.

Reality set in: "are we nuts?" How in the blessed name will we last on that long road, we all thought to ourselves. What will we pack…what kind of food will we take if we get hungry…will we have the right kind of gas to last for such a journey? All these problems will have to be solved before we go anywhere. We were really serious about this trip. We want to go visit the Kingdom of Heaven, absolutely. Somehow, God would have to know when we are coming and what time to expect our arrival. We won't know what the weather would be like, or where we would stay. We realize that Heaven is a very large wide-spread place; but we would have the difficult task of finding our Heavenly Father. It would be very important to find Him first to receive our instructions. The only thing we can do before our journey, would be to pray and send a message through our prayers so God can hear us and know that we would be there.

Through the spirit of Jesus, we could hear from Heaven the answers to our questions. On Earth, we were chosen for a purpose. God placed us on Earth to do His master plan. When God blessed us, He had others in mind for us to be a blessing to, which was His significant call. For the fulfillment of His purpose, we must be tied into the purpose by the counsel of the Lord. All of us should get involved to do His Kingdom work and maintain an agenda. The divine perspective must be God's prerogative—we can't choose the assignment; but can live it out and be rewarded for deliverance. God's unmerited favor is to save us. His grace will be made available to us, though we did not earn it. He sent the Holy Ghost and made many things available to us; but we did not obey. His salvation was healing, deliverance, soundness, safety and protection. God provides out of goodness for us to be obtained by our faith. He made a choice far beyond our careers; not just getting something for us only. Fed-up with our failure on Earth, we decided to rise to the next level and a new level. We must discover the good life. God will layout and design the blueprint for us to reach Heaven for everlasting life.

God will prepare a path because He knows that we love Him and His love for us is revealed by His spirit. We must repent for our earthly sins and look for that path. God will prepare paths ahead of time for us and pre-arrange and set-up the good life and make ready for us because He will be expecting us. If we choose to walk in that path, the path will be littered with good things. We will receive the fullness of joy, exceeding riches, gifts and pleasures forevermore, more than what we couldn't receive on Earth.

We all agreed that this would be a prime opportunity and there will be no "U-turn." No doubts in Heaven, for we will keep God's Commandments as He outlined to Moses in B.C.

My friends and I will devise a plan in preparation for our journey. We will paint our automobiles different colors, and have them numbered for identification on the special road. We were told that there were two roads; one would lead to destruction and the other will lead the path to Heaven. Of course, we knew which one we would travel and that's why it would become necessary for us to have identifying automobiles. There will be ten (10) automobiles on that path. Oh! How excited we were, knowing that soon we would be on the journey to a new life. We decided not to pack suitcases or food. We would just dress warmly in a sweat suit and sneakers; take bottles of water and wear depend diapers. We are not sure if there would be restrooms on that selected path. This would be quite an experience because we have never found anyone else who journeyed to Heaven and returned to tell us about it. We knew that we would be going on faith and remembrance of what we read in the Holy Bible.

Our plans were to fly to a centrally located city where it would be convenient to purchase these special automobiles. Everyone arrived safely that Friday night and checked into a hotel agreed by all in Rocky Mount, North Carolina. After a good nights' sleep, we rose early the next morning and searched the directory for a car dealership that would accommodate us for the purchase of ten (10) cars. Also, we would have to find a chop-shop that could paint the cars and number them without asking too many questions.

Perhaps we could convince them that we were going to enter into an "auto-race" event. We were convincing and got all the cars painted and numbered. The question now is where do we begin our convoy and what time shall we leave. We didn't stay another night and didn't want to be noticeable as being in a convoy with numbered cars. One of my friends from North Carolina knew the area well and suggested that we travel at night. She thought it might be wise to travel a rural road near the lakes. We were all set to go. We had an envisioned road map by the Spirit of God and we just faithfully followed that path. We were so excited.

Chapter 2

On The Road With My Friends

As we traveled the lakeside, darkness set in and it was getting chilly. We didn't think to bring a jacket or coat. We would just have to leave the car windows up. There was no thought of running out of gas, for we were on a mission to get to Heaven and believe that God would take care of us. The nights seemed long and dreary and sleep began to take over us. We all agreed to stop after a four hour travel. We had to sleep in our cars. We pulled on the side of the road and safely locked our doors and went to sleep. Daylight shined into our windshields and awakened us and we had to change our depends and continue our journey. We always traveled back roads near lakes, not to be noticed by possibly a policeman or would-be evil doers. We drank our water moderately, not to consume too much because we had no idea how far we had to travel before God would meet us. It seemed like forever that we were traveling. We have now been on the path for five days and nights; stopping only to change our depends. We were not tired at all and didn't complain to each other.

Something was happening in the Heavens after a ten day journey. We all stopped our cars and looked up into the Heavens. There was a message written in the sky that said: "you are to keep traveling the route you're on." We all shivered in dismay, and looked at each other pondering what would happen next. Again, we looked up into the Heavens, and each of our names were written. We were amazed to have learned that God knew us personally by name. We got back into our respective cars and resumed our journey. Two more days passed, but we kept driving on this very strange road that never had a stop sign or any traffic lights. We never could see another road parallel to the road we were traveling on. There were many other cars, large and small going the same direction as we were. We wondered if somehow, we would meet at a junction and we all will be traveling the same journey. After discussing this concern, we remembered that God said there would be two paths; one would lead to destruction and one would lead to Heaven. So we accepted the fact that we were on the path to Heaven and should not be concerned about the other cars. We were just to keep focused on where we were and being directed by God.

Early one night as we continued to travel, there was another message in the sky. Because it was night, the message was clearer to see by the naked eye which read: "you're on the right course, please do not make any turns and do not exit, for you will soon arrive, for I am waiting with open arms." We all got out of our cars and embraced each other, shed tears and sat down on the side of the road. There were no other cars traveling that road at that time. It was as if the road was designed just for us. After about a half hour, we all returned to our cars and preceded to follow the directions given us.

As we drove another two days, we were shocked to see ahead of us many ducks that looked like turkeys traveling on the side of the road. I stopped and peered out of the window to try and make out actually what they were. My friends were debating what kind of ducks could they be and why were they headed in the direction as we were. I thought surely they can't be headed to Heaven. How would they know the route and would they understand the spiritual language. Although there were about 50 or more of them, they made no sounds. Everything was quiet and serene as though they were meditating, or perhaps listening to someone or something. We all preceded to drive slowly alongside them just to see where they were going. After about thirty minutes or so, we were exhausted with the slow movement, so we just sped up and decided to continue our journey. I began to look back in the rear view mirror at the ducks until they were out of sight. I quickly pushed the thought out of my mind that they would really be headed to Heaven.

As we continued our journey, I began to second-guess my decision to take this trip. Although the world that I was leaving behind became very boring and a positive future was not in the making, I had to wonder what living in Heaven was going to be like. Would I find love for another human being? Would there be social events where I could attend or would there just be saints singing and praising the Lord?

Would there be sports, movies, concerts, politics and other things I like similar to the world I left behind? Would there be regular food for us or would we have to adjust to some unknown menus. I had dispel all those questions out of my head. I realized that Heaven would be nothing like life on Earth. It was time to stop and rest for a while. Everyone pulled on the side of the road to rest and discussed the decision we made to reach Heaven. Surprisingly, they were all excited about the trip and told me to stop having reservations and that we had come too far to turn around. The friend from North Carolina reminded all of us that we didn't belong back in time", that we belonged in eternity. Eternity was where there are no more delays or disappointments. The Earth really had plenty of disappointments and too many delays. She further expressed how unpredictable some men were and that they could not be trusted. The Florida friend shouted that she was so fed-up with men lying about not having other relationships, yet he could not make a commitment to her. My California friend told of her frustrations with the job market not being wide-spread. She said that there was so much favoritism in the work place and she would work so hard and for long hours, but never get the promotion she so much deserved. The girl that did less work, slacked in productivity, always favored by the boss, got all the recognition and promotion. We all agreed that, that was truly unfair. Who needs that kind of treatment, asked the friend from the Bahamas? The Bahamas friend moved to the Bahamas with her late husband just to get away from the hustle and bustle of racism and foreigners taking over jobs and businesses in the U.S. After the death of her husband, she no longer felt the security that her late husband provided for her while he was living.

She felt she was always being taken advantage of. The Alabama friend expressed how her relatives were always wanting to borrow money from her and never paid a cent back. Although she loved them so much, she welcomed the opportunity to hear from them because family mattered. It took quite a while for her to realize that they were playing on her kindness, but she was never truly loved by them. She thought, "what a jerk I had been to think she could buy love." My Virginia friend Virginia dealt with the cold and icy weather for years.

She didn't think that she could adjust to living anywhere else, in fear of connecting with the wrong people, meaning neighbors. Every winter, she had to shovel snow and deal with blizzards and snow storms. Unfortunately, she didn't have a car, but had to depend on rapid transit systems for her transportation around town. She had to do her grocery shopping during her travels, not wanting to do it on the weekends. This was done repeatedly week after week; but now, she would not have to deal with this drama and she felt relieved.

My Georgia friend had to deal with the crowded highways full of traffic day and night. When she thought she could get out early hours of the morning without having to be stuck in traffic, she discovered that traffic was jammed in the early hours as the mid-day or night hours. She found out that people did not have to report to work that early, but had to leave early to avoid the heavy flow of traffic, which would be exhausting and frustrating. In speaking with the New York friend, the subway trains were increasingly crowded with teenagers who were ignorant and disrespectful. Many times, they would relieve themselves in the corner of one of the compartments of the train, which left a very foul odor.

Security is not what it used to be; because of the increase in crime, security is afraid also. There was a time when anyone would feel very secure seeing officers frequent in all compartments of the train. She remembered having the luxury of reading novels during her travels to and from work, even if she had to stand and sway with the train. There was never a fear of having your purse stolen, or hearing a whole lot of profanity, nor feeling threatened by violence.

In Oklahoma, my friend felt very successful owning her own business as a realtor. After fifteen years of experience in the industry, she felt that she could influence people to buy their homes. Lately, there was a decline in the market for home-buying. After the Oklahoma bombing of the Federal Building which killed over one hundred sixty people or more, people began moving out of the area into other cities where they would feel safe. Back in the day, U.S. citizens never had to worry about terrorism on American soil. Today, everyone is constantly worried about it. Pennsylvania seemed to be the place to live. It has historical monuments, businesses and medical institutions. It is a cold city where many college students wanted to study and obtain the elite medical knowledge. The Albert Einstein Institute housed the most important science in history. Einstein developed ideas that changed people's views of the universe. She wishes there could be an Einstein Institute in Heaven.

Chapter 3

The Eagles' Nest

An end to our reminiscing, we decided to drink some water and continue our journey. Daylight peeled in after about three hours of driving. We passed by some mountains and saw what appeared to be an eagle sitting on her nest with her babies. It appeared to be looking down at us pass by, wondering where we were going. Somehow, it seemed that these animals that we began to see on our journey were positioned in our path to indicate that there will be no more people in sight. The eagle did not move at all; it just sat there looking down on us. The noise from our blowing our many horns did not frighten it at all.

The morning was cool, brisk, and refreshing. Perhaps the eagle would fly away after our convey of cars disappeared out of its sight. A few miles up the road, there it was. The eagle had stopped in the middle of the road.

We didn't want to run it over. My lead car kept blowing its horn for the eagle to move, but it wouldn't. I decided to take the chance and approach it to see if I could frighten it to fly away. As I extended my hands towards it, the eagle was not afraid of me. The eagle opened its mouth as if to say something that I could not understand. A very weird sound came out of its mouth. I didn't know what the sound represented. As I reached out again, the eagle leaped up into my arms and laid its head on my shoulder as though it needed to be nourished by me. All my friends got out of their cars and surrounded the eagle as I held it. I had no fear of this bird. I felt that there was some sort of message for us through this eagle.

After carefully examining the bird, we discovered a note in the beak of the eagle. I pulled the note out of its beak and something was scrolled in Arabic language. One of my friends translated it and didn't know what to do. The eagle held on tightly to me, not wanting me to let go. I took the eagle back to the car with me, sat it on the back seat and it released the hold on me, and I realized it was a female eagle. The other girls returned to their cars and we continued on our journey. For miles, the eagle made no sound at all. I wondered if it was thirsty, so I poured a little water from my bottle into the palm of my hand to let her drink some water. She was certainly thirsty and in searching for a cup, I found one. When I poured more water into the cup, the eagle drank it all. We had no food to eat because there was no urge to eat and water was just fine for our journey. Darkness was settling in and there were many clouds in the sky and the stars began to shine very bright. They were so bright that the sky literally lit up as though it was guiding us on our path. The eagle became restless seeing the brightness of the stars. The eagle began to make weird noises that caught my attention. She put her wing over her face as if the brightness of the stars bothered her. The female eagle flew out of the car heading back where we found her. I slammed on breaks and put the car in park, almost causing a chain reaction of an accident. All my friends trailing me slammed on their breaks as well; jumping out of their cars curious as to what was happening. My car followed the female eagle where she left her babies in the nest. The eagle brought her babies one-by-one to my car and laid each one on the back seat. To our amazement, there were nine more little eagles being born. My nine friends took one baby eagle each back to their cars, poured water from their water bottles, onto the babies to clean them up and to return them to their mother.

Water was all that we had to give the mother; and perhaps the water could produce some sort of substance to feed the babies. We were in total shock, not knowing what to make of the situation. As we sat there in the darkness of the night, we all looked up into the Heavens noticing that the stars had disappeared. The next thing we saw developing in the Heavens was a moon-like shape with green, red, blue and purple colors. Of course, we had no idea what it was.

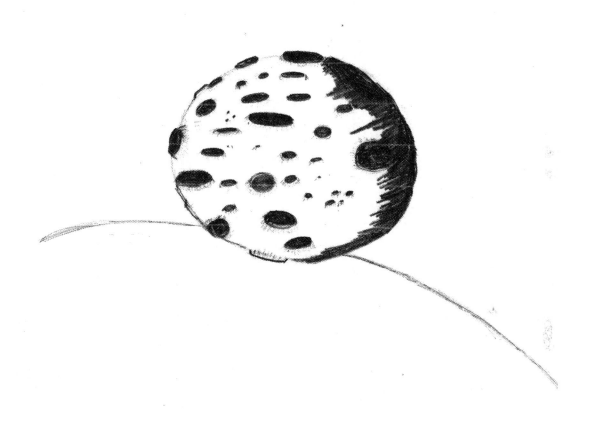

Suddenly, the mother eagle began making weird noises again in reaction to the symbol in the sky. Fear came over us and we couldn't explain our feelings of why we were afraid. I tried to calm the mother eagle down, and she snapped at me and bruised my hand. The bruise did not need medical attention. It's a good thing, because we didn't bring a first aid kit. We didn't anticipate getting injured on our way to Heaven. The symbol in the sky seemed to be coming closer to us and the eagle's noises got louder as if it were communicating with the symbol. We jumped back into our cars; but we did not drive off. We just sat there and watched the symbol.

The mother eagle became restless and lifted herself off of the babies. The babies scattered on the back seat and began making baby noises as the mother leaped around the inside of the car. I was afraid that the mother was going to break out the car window; so I rolled down all the windows so the mother could fly free into the night. The mother did fly out the window, leaving the babies behind. All the girls returned back to my car to see what was going on. The babies were restless like their mother and began squealing for their mother, who was no where to be found. Now, what are we to do with these babies? Soon, we were able to calm the babies down. We were frustrated, but preceded on our journey. However, we wondered how we would care for these baby eagles. After traveling a distance, the babies all went to sleep, and slept for hours. It was a pleasure to see them asleep. As morning broke, we all stopped the cars and allowed the baby eagles to get out and attempt to walk around the grounds and catch some fresh air. While attending to the babies, we were surprised to see their mother show up, flying through the air. The mother may not have been able to find us in the darkness; but certainly was able to see us at daybreak.

We were so happy to see her; if only she knew that her showing up was a real gift for us. One of my friends was able to find some straw in the bush and made a nest house for the babies. The mother eagle stood back patiently awaiting her babies to be placed in the nest house. As soon as they were all settled in, the mother sat over her babies to secure them. They all looked so peaceful and happy to see their mother. We backed up from the nest and returned to our cars and left the mother eagle caring for her babies. I personally did not want to look back in fear of the mother following us. I just kept focused on looking ahead and driving on towards our destination. I wondered how much longer was it going to take to get to Heaven. It was a sigh of relief for us all not to have extra luggage in our quest for a better life.

All the girls were getting restless and tired after being on the road over a week now. We were told that it could take at least a week and a half to reach Heaven. How could anyone know how long it would take. Only someone who had been to Heaven and back could predict the amount of time it would take. Is it possible that it could happen? One of the girls questioned why the eagle chose us to nourish her during her delivery of her babies. The weird noises were another concern of ours when the symbol appeared in the sky. The question that remained is what message the symbol gave the mother eagle. We wanted to know the answer; but who could give it to us. More and more, strange things began to happen on this journey.

Chapter 4

The Rapture Takes Place

The journey to Heaven was getting exciting and we were anxious to arrive. We were looking towards the universe. While living on Earth, we saw the stars in the sky, but we desperately wanted to see the different planets and all that existed in space. Curious about where we were at the moment, I stared in the Heavens and what appeared was an angels flying through the clouds and I was stunned. I had to blink my eyes several times to get a clear vision of what I had just seen. I knew that I was not dreaming, because I was still driving. Suddenly, I slammed on brakes, nearly hitting my head on the steering wheel. All my friends stopped before rear-ending each other. I jumped out of the car and pointed into the Heavens to my friends, and immediately, they all saw what I saw. We stared into the Heavens in delight, wondering if we were close to being taken up into the rapture. Fear came over us and we wondered if we would be lifted by the Angel one at a time. On Earth, we were made to believe that only God can take you up in the rapture. We only saw an Angel. The night was cool, and the sky was clear. We continued to stare into Heaven and kept our eyes on the Angel. When she came closer to us, she had on a beautiful white dress that looked like a robe.

Daryl Burchett

As the Angel was approaching us, one of my friends gasped for air, unable to breath. She appeared shaken and started to cry. We gathered around her to calm her down. She stated that she wanted to go back, remain on Earth; but we explained to her that we had come too far and there would be no turning around. Explaining to her that we were finally there, and needed to be strong, faithful and confident that God will take us up with the help of the angel. We told her that God would welcome us into His warm arms. She was asked if she believed in God and she replied: "Yes"; so I told her to just trust God and be of good courage. At that moment, we saw God speaking with the Angel, giving her instructions to take each one of us one-by-one.

Suddenly, the Angel came closer to us with open wings and a beautiful smile. Fearfully, all ten of us formed a circle and kneeled down to pray. The angel began singing a very soft tune that we were not familiar with. She had on a beautiful white seemingly robe with gold lace and her hair was very long and silky with a gold head band around her head. She was so beautiful and thinly shaped. She descended from the sky and landed on the ground where we were still praying. We didn't know what to say or do at that point. We just watched her in amazement. The Angel reached for my friend from North Carolina and took her by her arms. She took her up into the Heavens and as we watched, they disappeared through the clouds. There was no sound coming from her or my friend. The other of us looked fearful at each other. We were so stunned and said absolutely nothing. We started praying again and thought we should sing a song.

Shortly after praying and singing for nearly thirty minutes, the Angel re-appeared and took my friend from Philadelphia up into the Heavens and disappeared. One-by-one, we all were taken up into the Heavens.

We knew that Heaven would be a glorious place to live and where people go after dying on Earth; but we were alive and aware of our existence. We made it and now we will experience time without beginning and without ending.

AMEN

Conclusion

"When I consider thy Heavens, the work of thy fingers, the moon and the stars, which thou hast ordained; what is man, that thou art mindful of him? And the son of man, that thou visited him. For thou hast made him a little lower than the angels, and hast crowned him with glory and honor."

Psalm 8:3-5

AMEN

Printed in the United States
By Bookmasters